GW01228138

THE H·Y·P·N·O·T·I·S·E·R

THE
H·Y·P·N·OT·I·S·E·R

MICHAEL ROSEN

Pictures by Andrew Tiffen

ANDRE DEUTSCH

First published in 1988 by
André Deutsch Limited
105-106 Great Russell Street, London WC1B 3LJ

Copyright © 1988 by Michael Rosen
Illustrations copyright © 1988 by Andrew Tiffen
All rights reserved

British Library Cataloguing in Publication Data

Rosen, Michael, 1946-
   The hypnotiser.
   I. Title   II. Pinchuck, Tony
   821'.914   PR6068.068

   ISBN 0 233 97929 9

Phototypeset by Falcon Graphic Art Ltd
Wallington, Surrey
Printed in Great Britain by
WBC Print Limited

CONTENTS

Horrible	7	The Grinners Book of Records (2)	68
Cool Guy and Fool Guy	9	Box	69
Laura Singing	10	Me and My Brother	70
Tickle	12	Laura	72
My Project	13	The Project	74
Hot Food	14	Strict	78
The Hollywood	16	Great Moments in History (3)	79
The Car Trip	20	The Hypnotiser	80
Transport Test	22	Logic	84
London Airport	23	Playing with Words	84
Great Moments in History (1)	28	Felt Tip	85
Conversations with a Two Year Old (Laura)	29	George	86
Long Distance Phone Call: Michael to Geraldine	31	Conversation Between Three Children	87
The Outing	35	The Michael Rosen Rap	88
Tea-Time	40	No One In	90
The Grinners Book of Records (1)	41	Tidy Your Room	91
Babysitter	42	Puzzle I	92
A Ball	50	Puzzle II	92
Deep Down	50	Headache	92
Far Away	51	The Grinners Book of Records (3)	93
My Dad	51	I Think	94
Goldfish	52	Tomato 1	95
Fridge	54	Tomato 2: Or How I've Learnt to Love Tomatoes	98
Great Moments in History (2)	56	My Mum's Mum and My Dad's Dad	99
Hot Air	57	Quiet Please	100
Presents	58	Toe Nails	101
May	62	The Grinners Book of Records (4)	102
Christmas	66		

Telly	103	More Wise Words from Doctor	
Useless Information	104	Smartypants	116
My Mind Took Me	105	The Skyfoogle	117
Eileen	106	Shram and Shreddle	120
My Dad Calls Me	107	Great Moments in History (4)	121
I Went	108	Harrybo	122
Fast Food	109	The Bump	124
My Mum	114	Spots in my Eyes	125
Zoo Cage	114	Mistakes	126
Wise Words from Doctor		Laura and Dolly	128
Smartypants	115		

HORRIBLE

I was starving.
All I had for breakfast was
one apple and fifteen raisins.
It was half past twelve
and I had to get to Hemel Hempstead.
So I bought a pizza
and I ran and ran
and jumped on my train.

As we pulled out of Euston Station
I began to eat.
Trouble was:
my pizza was in a paper bag –
one
sloppy
cheesey
pizza
with the melting cheese and tomato
stuck
to the bag.

So I peeled the paper off my pizza
but it was all slippery and sticky
and the pizza came off in
soggy lumps
that I scooped together
and pushed into my mouth
blob
by
blob.

But there were dollops of pizza
hiding in the corner of the bag
so I was holding the bag up to my face
tipping it into my mouth
I was drinking pizza
and my fingers were running with
dribbles of tomato
and slops of spicy cheese
all over my knuckles.

So there I was licking at my skin
but my fingers were trailing all over my chin.
So off went my tongue round my face
hunting for drips of pizza
but a bit of paper bag
had got into my mouth
so I was in there trying to get it out
with the finger I was licking.
It was diving into the
slobber
in my mouth
and I was snuffling with my nose
like I was
breathing in
pizza.

It was then
I noticed
the woman opposite.
She was watching me.
She looked like
she had never seen anything
quite
so
horrible
in all her life.

COOL GUY AND FOOL GUY

Cool guy
met
fool guy
going down the street.

Said
cool guy
to
fool guy
who ya gonna meet?

Said
fool guy
to
cool guy
I don't want no meat.

Said
cool guy
to
fool guy
I mean meet not meat.

LAURA SINGING

When Laura sings songs
she stands in front of you
she opens her mouth really wide
she opens her eyes really wide
she opens her arms really wide
she takes in huge breaths
and out comes this huge sing-song sound
that goes on and on and on
in great waves
with hundreds of different words and noises:

HAPPY HAPPY
HAPPY BIRTHDAY CAKE
HAPPY BIRTHDAY CAKE
THE CAKE
THE CAKE
THE DOOR
AND THE DOOR
AND THE DOOR IS OPEN
MERRY MERRY MARY
MERRY MARY MERRY
MERRY MERRY
DA DEE DEE
DUBBA DEE DEE
NAOMI GO TO SCHOOL
YES
OH YES
MY PYJAMAS GO TO SCHOOL
PYJAMAS GO TO SCHOOL
MERRY MERRY MARY
THE DOLLY IS ON THE WATER
THE BOOK IS ON THE WATER
THE PAPER IS ON THE WATER
ON THE WATER
THE WATER
ON THE WATER

I WENT ON THE PHONE
I CALLED THE PHONE
I WENT IN THE TAR-TAR
I WENT IN THE BOO BOO
I WENT IN ANOTHER BOO
SHOP SHOPPING
SHOP SHOPPING
SHOP SHOPPING
I MAKE A PIZZA
THE PIZZA
MUCKY PIZZA
MUCKY PIZZA
PIZZA IN THE BATHROOM
I EAT THE BATHROOM
I EAT THE DOOR
I EAT THE BATH . . .
I tired now
I not sing anymore,
she says.
And we have to go,
hooray hooray lovely singing
and clap our hands
otherwise she will get angry with us.

TICKLE

When I tickle Laura on the back of her neck
she snorts and cackles
and giggles and gargles
and wheezes
her face creases up
she looks like she's going to burst
until she shouts:
NO MORE DADDO
NO MORE DADDO.

Everything goes quiet.

Then she says:

more kickle now Daddo.

My Project: TRANSPORT

Kinds of Transport

The Spaceship

The Plane

The Bicycle

The Foot

The Nose

HOT FOOD

We sit down to eat
and the potato's a bit hot
so I only put a little bit on my fork
and I blow
whooph whooph
until it's cool
just cool
then into the mouth
nice.
And there's my brother
he's doing the same
whooph whooph
into the mouth
nice.
There's my mum
she's doing the same
whooph whooph
into the mouth
nice.

But my dad.
My dad.
What does he do?
He stuffs a great big chunk of potato
into his mouth.
Then
that really does it.
His eyes pop out
he flaps his hands
he blows, he puffs, he yells
he bobs his head up and down
he spits bits of potato
all over his plate
and he turns to us and he says,
'Watch out everybody –
the potato's very hot.'

THE HOLLYWOOD

We went to this cafe
and I had loads to eat
I had cod and chips.
The cod was huge
and there were hundreds of chips.
Hundreds and hundreds of them.

And I ate the lot.

Then mum said,
'Anyone want any afters?'
And we looked to see what there was.
There was apple pie.
Don't like that.
There was jam roly poly.
Don't like that.
And there was ice cream.
I like that.

There was chocolate, strawberry and vanilla.
I was just about to say,
'I'll have a strawberry ice cream,'
when I saw something else.
It said:
THE HOLLYWOOD.

And it was
vanilla ice cream
peaches
cream
chocolate sauce
cherries
trifle
jelly
and
strawberry ice cream.

So I said,
'I'll have a Hollywood.'
Dad said,
'He won't eat it.
They're huge.'
But Mum said,
'No no no
if he wants it he can have it.'
Dad said,
'Waste of money.
He won't eat it.'
Mum said,
'A Hollywood please.'
And we waited.

Then suddenly it appeared.
On its own.
Right in the middle of a tray.
With a little paper umbrella stuck in the top.
Everyone in the cafe looked round:
'What's that?'
'That's the Hollywood.'
'Oh yes. That's the Hollywood all right.'

And the woman put it down.
In front of me.
THE HOLLYWOOD
With the little paper umbrella stuck in the top.
It was huge.
It was taller than me,
And I had this really long spoon
to eat it with,
and now
everyone was looking at me.

I had to reach up
to get to the cherry on the top.
Got it.
In the mouth.
It was lovely.
Then on to the ice cream
and the chocolate sauce.
Dig in.
That was a bit rich
but OK.
Dad loves ice cream and
chocolate sauce
and he's watching me . . .
but I don't give him any.

Then there was some jelly stuff
and actually
that wasn't very nice.
Actually —
it was horrible.
Dad said,
'Slowing down are you?'
Mum said,
'Leave him alone.'

Now I was filling my cheeks
so as not to taste it so much.
My hands went hot.
People were looking at me.

Then I got to the trifle.
Soggy cake.
And that was
even more horrible.
I couldn't bear it in my mouth.
I couldn't even put it in my cheeks.
I hunched my shoulders and
I spat some into my hand.
I stopped eating.

Dad said,
'Stopped have you?'
Mum said,
'Leave him alone.'
'I don't like it very much,'
I said.

Dad's hand darted across the table.
'I'll finish it,' he said.
You bet he said that.
'I'll finish it,' he says.

And Mum turned to me
and said,
'Never mind, dear.
You won't ask for one of those again,
will you?'

I don't suppose I will.

THE CAR TRIP

Mum says:
'Right, you two,
this is a very long car journey.
I want you two to be good.
I'm driving and I can't drive properly
if you two are going mad in the back.
Do you understand?'

So we say,
'OK, Mum, OK. Don't worry,'
and off we go.

And we start The Moaning:
Can I have a drink?
I want some crisps.
Can I open my window?
He's got my book.
Get off me.
Ow, that's my ear!

And Mum tries to be exciting:
'Look out the window
there's a lamp-post.'

And we go on with The Moaning:
Can I have a sweet?
He's sitting on me.
Are we nearly there?
Don't scratch.
You never tell him off.
Now he's biting his nails.
I want a drink. I want a drink.

And Mum tries to be exciting again:
'Look out the window
There's a tree.'

And we go on:
My hands are sticky.
He's playing with the doorhandle now.
I feel sick.
Your nose is all runny.
Don't pull my hair.
He's punching me, Mum,
that's really dangerous, you know.
Mum, he's spitting.

And Mum says:
'Right I'm stopping the car.
I AM STOPPING THE CAR.'

She stops the car.

'Now, if you two don't stop it
I'm going to put you out the car
and leave you by the side of the road.'

He started it.
I didn't. He started it.

'I don't care who started it
I can't drive properly
if you two go mad in the back.
Do you understand?'

And we say:
OK, Mum, OK, don't worry.

Can I have a drink?

TRANSPORT TEST.
Fill in the Gaps

A submarine is a boat that goes under **CARROTS**

A bicycle has a saddle and two **WINDOWS**

The first man to reach the South Pole was called **MADONNA**

In 1492, a man sailed to America he was called **CHRISTOPHER COLUMBUM**

A satellite is launched by a **PEANUT** and goes round and round the **SUPERMARKET**

LONDON AIRPORT

Once my brother said,
'Why don't we go to London Airport
for your birthday treat?
We could spend all day there.
London Airport. Looking at the planes.
It'll be great.'
'Yeah,' I said.
'It'll be great.'

Mum said yes
so we took sandwiches and chocolate
and drinks.
I was really looking forward to it.

When we got there
my brother found out
that there was this bus
that you could go on
a kind of trip round the runways
so you could get right close up to the big jets.
Great.
Really great.
So he got the tickets
and we got on to the bus.

As we were getting on,
I said,
'Brian, I want a wee.'
So he goes,
'Well you can't now.
This is the last bus today
it's just about to go
we won't get on another one.'

'Brian,' I said,
'I want a wee.'
So he goes,
'You can't, you can't now
it'll wait
it's not that long a time to wait.'

So we got on,
the bus started up
and away we went.
The driver starts going,
'We're coming to runway four now.
If you look out to your right
you can see two planes . . .'
'I'm dying for a wee,' I said.
'It'll go away,' says my brother.
'I want a wee,' I said.
'What's the matter?' said the man in front.
'He wants a wee,' said my brother,
'You can wait, can't you?' said the man.
'No,' I said.
'Well don't do it here, will you?' he says.
'Can we stop the bus?' I said.
'Don't be daft,' says my brother,
'we're on the end of runway four.
You can't do a wee on the end of runway four.'

And the bloke driving the bus goes:
'If you look out of your window
you can see a baggage truck . . .'
'I'm going to wet myself,' I said.
My brother says,
'Look, there's Concorde,
just think of something else.'
'I can't,' I said,
'it's hurting.
I've got to do it
I've got to do it.'

The bus went on
We saw more planes
and more planes
and more planes
and more planes.

'You haven't wet yourself, have you?'
my brother says.
'No!'
More planes
more planes
more planes
'Here goes,' I said.

Then the bus stopped.
I rushed off the bus
I got to the toilet
and everything was lovely once again.
Wonderful.

And then we went home.

Mum said,
'Did you have a good time?'
And my brother said,
'It was great. Really great.'
'And how about you?' she said to me.
'How was your birthday treat?'
'All right,' I said,
'all right.
but . . .
but I wanted a wee
and they wouldn't let me.'

And then I cried.

GREAT MOMENTS IN HISTORY

The First Landing on the Moon.

The picture we saw......

The picture we didn't see.....

CONVERSATIONS WITH A TWO YEAR OLD, (LAURA)

Do you want an apple?
No.
What do you want, then?'
An apple.

★ ★ ★ ★

Do you want something to eat?
No.
Do you want some puffed wheat?
Yes.

★ ★ ★ ★

What are you doing?
Got my pockets in my hands.

★ ★ ★ ★

Hallo, Laura.
Hallo, Eddie, what's your name?
Eddie.
No tisn't. It's Joe.

★ ★ ★ ★

What's the time?
Twenty four hours ago.

★ ★ ★ ★

Go wash your hands in the bathroom.
My hands aren't in the bathroom.

★ ★ ★ ★

What's the matter?
I got a headache in my foot.

★ ★ ★ ★

Now what's the matter?
I got a tummyache in my head.

★ ★ ★ ★

Are you all right?
I done saw a funny noise.

LONG DISTANCE PHONE CALL: MICHAEL TO
GERALDINE.

GERALDINE SPEAKING:

Hallo, lovely of you to ring.

NAOMI SIT DOWN

Where are you now?
Oh nice. Have you got a telly in your room?

NO, YOU'RE NOT WATCHING TELLY NOW. IT'S BED
TIME

No, not you, you fool, you can go to bed anytime you like.
It's been absolutely terrible here. I'm shattered.

PUT IT DOWN LAURA. PUT IT DOWN. NAOMI HELP
HER

Would you believe it? She can see I'm on the phone and she
can't even help Laura with her corn flakes . . .

AND NOW IT'S ALL OVER THE FLOOR, YOU FOOL.

Of course it's not your fault, Michael.
So. Have you been busy?

NAOMI, COULDN'T YOU SEE IT?

She stood in it. Right in it.

THEY'RE ALL OVER YOUR SHOE, GIRL.
DON'T BE SO CLUMSY.
CAN'T YOU SEE I'M ON THE PHONE. JUST PLAY WITH
   HER
KEEP HER HAPPY

You sound ever so far away.
Yes, I suppose Singapore is a long way away now I think of it.

TAKE HER AWAY FROM IT.
I DON'T WANT HER TO PRETEND TO DO THE
   WASHING UP IN IT.
NAOMI, CAN YOU HEAR ME?
I DON'T WANT HER TO WASH UP WITH THE
   CORNFLAKES

The builders have made a terrible mess with the wall.

NOT ON ME, LAURA.

You know what she's done? Yes. All down my skirt.
I can't describe it.
Oh, you mean the wall.
No I can't describe that either.

NAOMI, QUICK TAKE HER THERE IF SHE WANTS TO
   GO.
NO, MUMMY CAN'T TAKE YOU, LAURA. I'M ON THE
   PHONE.
GO ON TAKE HER THERE, NAOMI. YOU'VE DONE IT
   BEFORE, HAVEN'T YOU?
JUST SIT HER ON IT AND STAY WITH HER

Would you believe it, she won't go unless I take her.
Look, it's lovely of you to ring.

STOP SCREAMING. I CAN'T HEAR A WORD MICHAEL'S
   SAYING

What do you mean the hotel collapsed?
Oh no, she's done it.

NAOMI, YOU COULD HAVE TRIED.
LAURA, YOU KNOW THAT'S NAUGHTY
YOU KNOW NOT TO DO IT ON THE FLOOR

Did you say collapsed?

A CLOTH. A CLOTH. ANY CLOTH. A KITCHEN TOWEL. A PAPER HANKIE.
ANYTHING, NAOMI.

She behaves like she's never spilt anything in her life,
my mother would have tanned the backside off me if I behaved like her, you know.
Not *your* hotel?

I'LL TELL YOU WHAT HE SAYS IN A MINUTE.
YOU DO WHAT YOU'VE GOT TO DO
AND LEAVE ME TO TALK TO MICHAEL
WAIT LAURA

Can you hear? Isn't that sweet?
Laura wants to say hallo.

LET LAURA SAY HALLO FIRST, NAOMI

She's tried to snatch it off Laura.

REALLY, NAOMI. THINGS LIKE THAT MAKE HER SCREAM.
NOW SAY HALLO TO DADDO, LAURA.
MIND THE CORNFLAKES . . . TOO LATE. NEVER MIND

She says she doesn't want to say hallo to fatbum.
Look, are you all right?
What was it, an earthquake or something?
Hallo?
Hallo?
Hallo?

Hallo?

THE OUTING

Right class 6
RIGHT CLASS 6
I'm talking

I'm talking
I want complete quiet
and that includes you, David Alexander,
yes you
no need to turn around, David
there aren't any other David Alexanders here are there?
Louise
it isn't absolutely necessary for your watch
to play us London's Burning just now, is it?

Right
as you know
it was our plan to go out today –
to the Science Museum.
Now I had hoped that it would not be necessary
for me to have to tell you –
yes, you as well, Abdul,
you're in class 6 as well, aren't you?
I saw that, Mark,
I saw it.
Any more and you'll be out.
No trip,
nothing.

I had hoped that it wouldn't be necessary
for me to tell you how to BEHAVE
when we go on a trip.

But –
and this is a big but –
you haven't heard a word I've said, have you, Donna?
This is a big but
I HAVE to tell you how to behave, don't I?
Why?

Yes, it IS because you never listen
but there's another reason, isn't there?
Yes, Warren,
because of what happened last time.

Let us remind ourselves of a few things:
The food –
Even as I speak
would you believe it?
I can see that Phanh has opened her can of drink
I do not believe it
I really don't.
Do we have lunch at nine-thirty at school?
No,
we have lunch at 12:15
but, Phanh, you've already begun yours.
If you remember,
last time
Joanna had eaten all her sandwiches
before she even got to school.
Lloyd sat on his orange
and burst it
and Alfred put a chocolate swiss roll in his pocket
and –
yes –
it melted.

So remember lunch is when?
yes yes yes
of course lunch is at lunch time
but when?
12:15
correct

Perhaps, I thought,
when I got up this morning
I won't have to tell class 6
about what to do when we get to the station
but then I remembered
David's little gang
who decided they wouldn't wait for me to tell them
what train to get on
and before we all knew it
David and his little gang
were heading for the sea-side on their own.

When we get to the museum –
Of course YOU'RE not listening, are you, Lydia?
But then of course you didn't listen last time, did you?
And then you wondered why
you sat on Lloyd's orange after Lloyd had already sat on it
    once.

When we get to the museum
do we run about the corridors?
Do we run around screaming?
Do we go sliding on the shiny floors?
No we don't
no we don't
no we don't.

Thank you, Mervyn, that's enough
I'm very glad you've got jam in your sandwiches, Mervyn,
we are all glad that you've got jam in your sandwiches,
     Mervyn,
but what has it got to do with sliding on the floor of the
     Science Museum?
Precisely nothing.
I'm very sorry, Mervyn, but nobody,
nobody at all
wants to know about the jam in your sandwiches, Mervyn.

Now,
when you're ready
when you're quiet
we'll all go.
That doesn't mean leaping up in the air, Karen,
does it?
Louise, why is your watch now playing
For He's A Jolly Good Fellow?
Yes, I know it could be SHE'S A Jolly Good Fellow, Zoe,
but that isn't what we are talking about, is it?

Mervyn,
if I hear about your sandwiches
your jam
or the jam IN your sandwiches
if I hear about any of it once more
I shall give them to the ducks.

Yes, John, what do you want?
I don't know what ducks, John.
Any ducks.

Right
when there is complete quiet
complete quiet
you will find your partners and stand by the door.

Oh no, not another chocolate swiss roll, Alfred,
surely not?

Marcia, you cannot have Charmaine AND Donna
as your partner
because that makes three
and three does not mean PARTNER, does it?
And perhaps you can put your comb in your bag for at least
   three seconds
just giving us enough time to get to the door? Mmm?

Good
right class 6 we're off

Why not leave your watch behind, Louise?

TEA-TIME

It's tea-time
and we're sitting at the table
and
my dad wants milk in his tea.

'Could you get me the milk?' he says.
I get the milk
I sit down again.

Then he wants butter for his bread.

'Could you get me the butter?' he says.
I get the butter
and I sit down again.

Then he wants a tea-spoon for his tea.

'Could you get me a tea-spoon?' he says,
and then my mum says,
'Once you get that bum of yours
stuck in a chair
you never get it off again, do you?'

And my dad says,
'I can't get a moment's peace round here.'

THE GRINNERS BOOK OF RECORDS

The worlds loudest Burp was produced in 1968 by James Carpetcleaner. It measured 9 on the Richter Scale.

WHAT YOU HAVE JUST WATCHED WAS A LIE

BABYSITTER

Sometimes my mum and dad used to go out.
This meant that my brother had to babysit me.

He hated it,
because I just wouldn't go to bed
when he told me to.
He was four years older than me.
(Actually he still is).
He'd shout
he'd rant and rave
WILL YOU GO TO BED!
But I never went
until I heard the front door open
with Mum and Dad
coming back.
And then
I'd be up the stairs
in a flash.

Anyway,
after a few months of this
my mum and dad tried something new.
Just before they went out
they said,
'Right Mick.
You go to bed before we
go out
AND
YOU
STAY
THERE.
'OK,' I said, 'OK OK OK,'
and off I went to bed.
I lay there waiting to hear the front door close.
SLAM.
And straightaway
Iwas
outthebed
downthestairs
intomybrother'sroom.

There he is
sitting there reading.
First of all he tries
I'm-not-taking-any-notice-of-Michael.
He goes on reading.
I think:
I'll make him take notice.
I put my face
behind the book
with my eye just peeping round the edge of the page.
Every time he gets to the end of a line
his eye looks into my eye.
He tries to pretend I'm not there.
It's no good.
He can't.
My eye is peeping away like mad
round the edge of his book.
He starts to laugh.

'Look,' he says,
'this
is
NOT
FAIR.
You promised you'd stay in bed
I'll tell them.
I'll tell them.
I will.'

So now I go and stand by the door
and I fiddle.
I make little rattly noises with the handle and the key.
Fiddle diddle
riddle diddle.
He tries to pretend I'm not there.
It's no good.
He can't.
I'm rattling away like mad
with the handle and the key.
He starts to laugh.

'Right,' he says,
'right,
that's it.'
He sounds like he's going to really do for me.
So now
he tries:
I'm-going-to-be-so-boring
Michael-will-get-so-fed-up-
he'll-go-back-to-bed.
He starts up a chant:
'Gotobed gotobed gotobed gotobed gotobed gotobed gotobed
   gotobed gotobed . . .'
He doesn't stop
'. . . gotobed gotobed gotobed gotobed gotobed gotobed
   gotobed gotobed gotobed gotobed . . .'
It goes on for ages.

I try to talk to him:
'What do you want for your birthday?'
'. . . gotobed gotobed gotobed gotobed gotobed gotobed . . .'
'Do you want a sweet?'
'. . . gotobed gotobed gotobed gotobed gotobed . . .'
'You've got a pimple on the end of your nose.'
'. . . gotobed gotobed gotobed gotobed gotobed gotobed . . .'

I'm still fiddling with the door.
I lock it
I unlock it
I lock it
I try to unlock it.

'. . . gotobed gotobed gotobed gotobed . . .'
I
can
not
un
lock
the
door.
I say,
'Brian . . . er . . . I can't . . . er . . .
the key's stuck.'

Suddenly he looks pleased.
He smiles to himself
and settles down with his book
and waits.

Meanwhile
I've got
BIG BIG BOTHER

. . . they're going to come back
and find me here
and I've got out of bed
and I've locked the door
and it's really late
and it's all my fault.

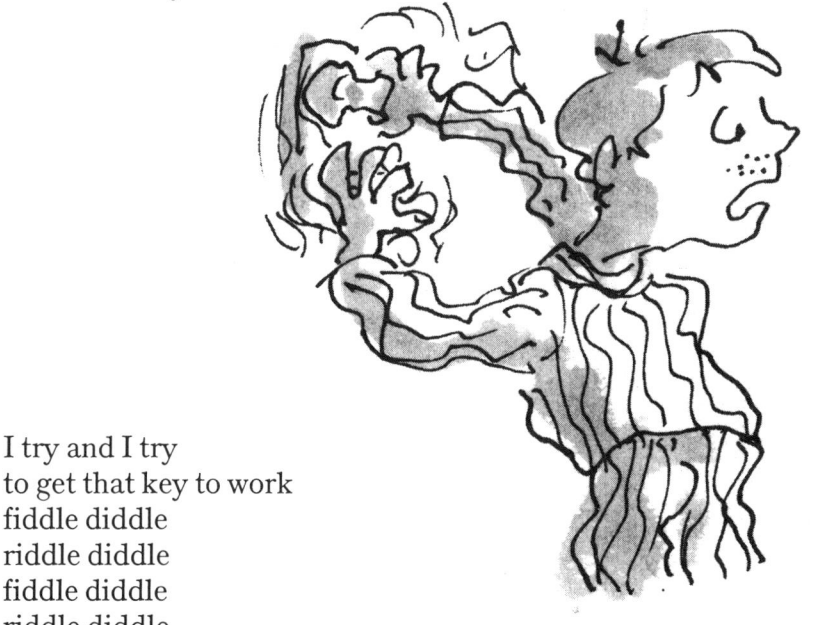

I try and I try
to get that key to work
fiddle diddle
riddle diddle
fiddle diddle
riddle diddle.

For three hours I'm at it.
And all the time
my brother is
not-taking-any notice-of-Michael.

The front door opens.
'Hallooo,' calls out my mum.
She gets to my brother's door.
'Did Michael stay in bed all right?'
She's trying to turn the handle.

'Let us in, Brian,' says my dad cheerily.
No answer from us inside.
My brother is waiting for me to say something
I'm hoping *he*'ll say something.
We're looking at each other.
'Come on,' says my dad
getting a bit cross.

Oh no, the moment I dread
when Dad goes from being cheery to
Absolutely Furious.

In a small weedy little voice
I say,
'I   locked   the   door.'

That really winds them up.
There's my mum,
'. . .Is that you, Michael?
. . .you still up?
. . .you promised you'd stay in bed
. . .it isn't fair on Brian.'

There's my dad
And he is roaring.
'. . .Would you believe it?
. . .the little pig
. . .and the door's jammed
. . .I'll have to break it down
. . .my god, when I get the other side
he'll get a good hiding.'

Me
I'm standing there
all shaky and sorry and shuddery.

But my brother
what's he doing?
He's smiling all over his big fat face.

He took the key out
passed it under the door
and they opened it.

I dashed out
and off to bed
fasterthananElectronicRabbit.

A BALL

Laura laughs
if she sees a ball bounce

I don't think it's funny

I wonder if
I used to laugh
at a ball bouncing
when I was two
like Laura.

If I used to laugh
why did I stop?

DEEP DOWN

deep down
where I don't know
deep down
inside
there's a place
so sad
such a sad sad place

sometimes it fills up
and it fills up
and it fills up
and overflows in my eyes
and all of me is so sad
such a sad sad place

FAR AWAY

I want to tell you about a place
I went
far far away

I sat on the grass
with someone there

I sat on the grass
with someone who loved me

I've never seen her again

and I don't think

I'll ever see that place I went
far far away

MY DAD

My dad says:

after the war was over
everyone came home
to sort things out

there weren't going to be any more wars
there weren't going to be any more poor people
there weren't going to be any more bad houses
there weren't going to be any more people out of work

that was forty years ago

now they're trying to invent space ships
that drop bombs.

GOLDFISH

On Monday
my dad woke me up.
'Wake up, wake up,' he shouts.
'Your goldfish is dead.'
I rushed over to the tank.
It wasn't dead,
it was just one of his tricks.

On Tuesday
my dad woke me up.
'Wake up, wake up,' he shouts.
'Your goldfish is dead.'
I rushed over to the tank.
It wasn't dead,
it was just one of his tricks

On Wednesday
my dad woke me up.
'Look, wake up – ' he says, dead quietly.
'Your goldfish is dead.'
'Oh no it isn't,' I said.
'Look, it is,' he said.
'Oh no it isn't,' I said.
'Look, it really is,' he said.

So I got up
and there was my goldfish
stuck on its side
on the top of the water
mouth open
eyes staring
tail stiff
dead in my tank.

It wasn't one of his tricks.

FRIDGE

Once I went to the fridge –
saw our jug in there
and I thought:
what's in it?
A syrup
what syrup?
Smell it – smells nice
finger in – lick it –
tastes nice
lift the jug and drink a bit
this is good
this is peach syrup
tinned peach syrup
what a drink!
So I drank the lot.

Not long after – a few days later
I went to the fridge
saw our jug in there
what's in it?
A syrup
what syrup?
Smell it.
O yes this is peach syrup again
lift the jug and drink some
drink some more, drink some more
drink the lot.

Not long after – a few days later
I went to the fridge
saw our jug in there
what's in it?
A syrup – yes!
Here we go again
lift the jug and fill my mouth
with that thick sweet juice . . .

Uckg!

This isn't peach
this is uckg
my mouth is full of oil
thick cooking oil

I wonder who put that there. . .

GREAT MOMENTS IN HISTORY

The Conquest of Everest.

The picture we saw ....

The picture we didn't see, five minutes before......

HOT AIR

I like it when you go to those places
where they have those hot air things
to dry your hands.

You press the silver button
the machine starts roaring
and hot air rushes out of a silver spout.

You hold your hands under it
and the water just dries off your hand.

Some of them,
you can turn the spout
and make it blow your hair about.

If you turn the spout round,
when your friends come in
they go to dry their hands
and the hot air goes
whooosh
into their face
whoooosh.
Warms your nose up, that does.

PRESENTS

I gave my mum and dad
all kinds of Christmas presents.

I used to go round the shops
for hours
looking at razors, key-rings,
clothes-brushes, bath-salts,
chocolate-gingers and so on.

Once I thought I had made a breakthrough.
I was at Salmon's the ironmongers
and there they were:
two jug things,
they were both made of glass
except for the tops.
One was a milk jug
and it had a bright green plastic top
and there was a little lever on it.
When you pulled the lever
a little door slid open
and you poured your milk out through
the little door.

The other jug was for sugar –
this one had a bright green plastic top as well
but this one was a kind of funnel
so you could pour the sugar out.
But it wasn't any old kind of funnel
It was special.
It had a little gadget inside the funnel
so you only poured out one teaspoonful at a time.
Magic.
So I bought these wonderful things
and gave them to my mum and dad for Christmas.

They said they were very nice.
They were very pleased.
And for a week or so after Christmas
they were always on the table.
If anyone wanted any milk or sugar
I'd say,
"Can I do it for you?
Do you want milk in your tea?
Let me do it."
And I rushed to pick up the jug
pull back the lever
and the milk poured out of the trap door.

Sugar?
And I picked up the sugar-jug
tipped it up
to pour out the magic one teaspoonful.
Another spoonful?
And I poured out the second one.
Anyone else?

I became the milk and sugar king.
I had to be the milk and sugar driver
all week I was pouring for everyone
breakfast, dinner, tea.

After a week or two
I noticed that the milk bottle was getting back
on to the table.
No jug.
I noticed the sugar bowl
and the boring old spoon
were getting back on to the table.
No sugar jug.

You see
someone had to fill those two jugs.

So I said
I'll do it
I'll get the new jug, eh?
I'll get the sugar thing
if you want? OK? Eh?

So I poured the milk and the sugar
into the jugs
and put them on to the table.

The only trouble was
they had got their milk and sugar by then.
They didn't need me to drive
their milk and sugar for them
my reign as the milk and sugar king was over.
I was beaten by the bottle and the bowl.

My bright green plastic topped jugs
went up on top of the kitchen cupboard
with the jam jars without lids.

We left them there
when we moved from that house.
They're probably still there.

MAY

A woman called May
used to look after us sometimes.
Her husband was a bus-conductor
and he could wink with both eyes.
Fantastic.
We used to meet him on his bus
and when we got our tickets off him
if we were lucky
he'd wink one eye, then wink the other eye
again and again
really fast.
Fantastic.

But best was
May,
when she came over.
After tea,
we played games.

My favourite was
Raisins.
This is how we played Raisins.

We tipped the raisins
out of the raisin jar
and we each guessed
how many raisins there were.

148, I'd say.
231, May said.
Then we took one raisin each
counting.
I take one – "One"
and put it in my mouth.
May takes one – "Two"
and she puts it in her mouth.
I take one – "Three"
into my mouth
May takes one – "Four"
in her mouth
and so it went on.
131 – in my mouth
132 – in her mouth.

I love raisins
all chewy and sweet
mmmmm
201 – in my mouth
202 – in May's mouth
203 – last one – in my mouth.

May had guessed best.
She had guessed 231.

But now
we had eaten all the raisins.
They were all gone.
The jar was empty.
Could be trouble.

Anyway,
then it was bedtime.

At tea-time the next day
we were having fruit salad
and my brother said:
"I'll have raisins on this."
He went to the cupboard
and he saw the empty jar
and he goes,
"Where have all the raisins gone?
The jar was full yesterday.
Mum, he's eaten them all.
Look at his face – you can see
he's eaten them.
Tell him off, Mum.
Tell him off."

And Mum says to me,
"Did you eat them?"
And I say,
"Me and May did."

And my brother says,
"See I told you.
It's not fair, Mum.
He's a greedy little pig."

And then a picture came into my mind
of the night before
of me and May
counting the raisins in our mouths
all chewy and sweet
mmmm
So I said,
"I'm not a greedy little pig."
And Mum said to my brother,
'Raisins don't last all week, you know."

But I didn't tell anyone
about our game,
Raisins.
203 – mmmmm . . .

CHRISTMAS

It was Christmas Eve.
I knew Father Christmas
was Mum and Dad.
I knew he didn't come down the chimney
and instead
they came through the door.
I knew it didn't all come out of a sack
but instead
they left a heap of stuff at the end of the bed.
I knew it, I knew it, I knew it.
What I didn't know
was what was going to be in the heap.

But I went to sleep.
So then I woke up.
Nothing.

So I went to sleep.
So then I woke up.
Nothing.
Was that piece of paper there before?
Must have been.

So I went to sleep.
So then I woke up.
Nothing.
And it's morning.

Has Father Christmas forgotten me?
I mean, Mum and Dad.

Get up.
Feeling bad.
Feeling worse than bad.
Terrible.
Nearly crying.

That piece of paper
what is it?
It's a picture of a bike
and underneath it, it says,
DOWNSTAIRS.

So it's rush-rush downstairs,
front room
and there it was
propped up against a chair,
in front of the telly.
Big and shining.
The bike.

Of course,
Father Christmas couldn't stuff a bike
down the chimney, could he?

THE GRINNERS BOOK OF RECORDS

The worlds most interesting freckle was discovered on Simon Wrigglestones bum in 1954.

The worlds noisiest hamster is Benny who lives with his owner Jenny in Hackney.

BOX

I made a box
with a lid and locks
big enough for me to sit in.

I took the chance
climbed in
and bolted the lid
above me.

I'd made the walls of my box
so that they could move in towards me.
The sides and the top
could come closer
and closer towards me
simply by my turning a handle
from the inside of my box.

Now that I was inside
with the lid shut
I turned the handle
and the box closed on me.
I could feel the bolts in the walls
digging into my skin.
I could feel my neck
being squashed down.
I felt like clothes in a suitcase,
my arms binding my body up.
I stopped still
feeling the feeling of it.
Look what I have made for myself.

Look what I am doing.

Look at the box
though you won't see me.
I'm on the inside.
Walnut in its shell.

ME AND MY BROTHER

Me and my brother,
we sit up in bed
doing my dad's sayings.
I go to bed first
and I'm just dozing off
and I hear a funny voice going:
'Never let me see you doing that again.'
and it's my brother
poking his finger out just like my dad
going:
'Never let me see you doing that again.'
And so I join in
and we're both going:
'Never
let
me
see
you
doing
that
again.'

So what happens next time I get into trouble
and my dad's telling me off?
He's going:
'Never let me see you doing that again.'
So I'm looking up at my dad
going,
'Sorry dad, sorry,'
and I suddenly catch sight of my brother's big red face
poking out from behind my dad.
And while my dad is poking me with his finger
in time with the words:

'Never
let
me
see
you
doing
that
again,'
there's my brother doing just the same
behind my dad's back
just where I can see him
and he's saying the words as well
with his mouth without making a sound.
So I start laughing
and so my dad says,
'AND IT'S NO LAUGHING MATTER.'
Of course my brother knows that one as well
and he's going with his mouth:
'And it's no laughing matter.'
But my dad's not stupid.
He knows something's going on.
So he looks round
and there's my brother
with his finger poking out
just like my dad
and I'm standing there laughing.
Oh no
then we get into
REALLY BIG TROUBLE.

LAURA

Baby Laura's the youngest in our house.
There's her sister called Naomi
she calls her
Maymee.
There's her mum
who she calls
Mum.
There's me
she calls Daddo, (though I'm not her real dad)
and there's my two boys, Joe and Eddie
who live with me for half the week
and live with their mum for the other half of the week.
Laura calls
Joe,
Doe
and she calls Eddie,
Deddie.
So there you have it
Mum, Daddo, Maymee, Doe and Deddie.

At bedtime she has to kiss us all good night.
Ny ny, she says
Ny ny
and she pushes out her lips
to make a kiss
and round she goes,
Maymee, Doe, Deddie, Daddo and Mum,
though sometimes she jumps into Joe's bed
and pretends she's asleep in there.
Yesterday she stuffed a little plastic camel
in the place where the tapes go in the video.
So the video doesn't work anymore.
Maybe she thought that if you put a plastic camel in there
the machine will copy it and
more plastic camels will come out.
The other day she got into the shopping
and started crunching up the weetabix all over the floor
and then mixing it with the eggs.
Maybe she thought she was cooking weetabix omelettes.
You can never tell what she's thinking.

THE PROJECT

At school
we were doing a
project.

You know the kind of thing:
THE VIKINGS –
TRANSPORT –
WOOD –

My son Joe
has done THE VIKINGS three times.
He did
STREETS
last term,
and the teacher didn't even take them into
a street.
He did
A VIEW OUT OF THE WINDOW
without even looking out of the window.

Our project was
HOLLAND.

There we were
reading:
'My friend Hans from Holland'
and we made windmills
and stuck blue strips of paper
on to white strips of paper.
They were canals.
And we kept talking about tulips
and cheese.
In the end
I thought they grew cheese
and ate tulips.

Then suddenly one day
our teacher
Miss Goodall
said that there was an inspector coming in.
She said he wasn't going to inspect us.
He was going to inspect her
and we were all to help her
by being really good
and answering all the questions that he asked us.

Later that day he came in.
He had a moustache.
We behaved.
Miss Goodall behaved.
There we all were
sitting in our rows
behind our desks
breathing very very quietly
and he looked at our windmills
and our canals
and he said:
What do they eat in Holland?
And I didn't put my hand up
in case I said tulips
but Sheena Maclean said cheese
and he said:
What do they grow in Holland?
and I didn't put my hand up for that one either
but Margot Vane said tulips.

And he asked some more questions
and we were doing really well.
Miss Goodall was trying very hard
not to look proud
and then he asked:
Who is the queen of Holland?

There was silence.

No one knew who was the queen of Holland.

Miss Goodall frowned
and started looking all round the class
with her eyes looking all hoping.

Then suddenly I remembered this funny little rhyme
that Harrybo used to say.

I put up my hand.

Yes, said the inspector.

Queen Juliana
is a fat banana,
I said.

Miss Goodall looked awful.
Harrybo was sitting in front of me
and I saw him snort and start giggling.

What did you say? said the inspector.
Queen Juliana, I said.
Good, he said.
You're right, quite right.
Miss Goodall was delighted
I was delighted.
The inspector was delighted.
and Harrybo was still snorting away like mad.

STRICT

Maybe you think you have a teacher
who's really strict
maybe you know a really strict teacher.
But when I was at school
we had a teacher who was so strict
you weren't allowed to breathe in her lessons.
That's true, we weren't allowed to breathe.
It was really hard to get through
a whole day without breathing.
Lips tightly shut.
Face going red.
Eyeballs popping out.
She'd go round the class glaring at us
and then she'd suddenly catch sight of one of us
and she'd yell
NO BREATHING, DO YOU HEAR ME? NO BREATHING.
And you had to stop breathing rightaway.
The naughty ones used to try and take quick secret breaths
under the table.
They'd duck down where she couldn't see them
snatch a quick breath and come back up
with their mouth shut tight.
Then someone would say,
'Excuse me, miss, can I go outside and do some breathing?'
And she'd say,
'WHAT? CAN'T YOU WAIT. YOU'VE HAD ALL
    PLAYTIME
TO BREATHE HAVEN'T YOU?'
And then she'd ask someone a question
like, 'Where's Tibet?'
and someone'd put up their hand and say
'Er . . . it's –'
and she'd be right in there with:
'YOU'RE BREATHING. I SAW YOU BREATHE.'
'I wasn't, miss, really I wasn't.'
'WELL YOU ARE NOW, AREN'T YOU?'
It was terrible.
She was so strict . . .

GREAT MOMENTS IN HISTORY

The Pyramids...

500 B.C.

2,500 B.C.

THE HYPNOTISER

Once a boy called Richard came to school
and said,
'I can hypnotise people.'
So we said,
'Yeah yeah, I bet you can't.'
So he said,
'OK. Playtime.'

So, playtime,
we all went on to the playground
and he said,
'Right, who wants a go?'
So Trevor said,
'Yeah, me.'
So this boy, Richard,
made Trevor lie down on the ground
on his back
and he took this gold ring
out of his pocket
and he put it very carefully
between Trevor's eyes
on the bridge of his nose.

Then Richard took this conker
out of his pocket.
It was on the end of a string.
Then he starts swinging the conker
to and fro in front of Trevor's eyes
and he starts up talking in this spooky voice,
'Watch the conker, watch the conker,
go to sleep, go to sleep,
watch the conker, watch the conker
go to sleep, go to sleep,'
and it went on for ages
and we were all crowding round
dead quiet
watching Trevor
lying on the ground
listening to Richard going,
'Go to sleep, go to sleep.'
'Is it working?' we said.
'Is he going to sleep?'
'He's hypnotised.'
'Blimey.'

Suddenly the going-in bell went.
At that, Trevor,
he goes and stands up.
He just stands up
and dusts himself down.
So we all crowd round him,
going,
'Were you asleep?'
'You were asleep, weren't you, Trev?'
'Hey, were you hypnotised?'
And he looks at us,
all fed up,
and he says,
'Only thing that happened
was, I got a ROTTEN HEADACHE.'

So after that
we used to go round telling people,
'You see that bloke over there,
him, Richard, he's brilliant.
He can hypnotise people.
He's a hypnotiser, you know.'
And Richard, he'd hear us saying all this
and he'd go,
'Oh come off it, you lot,
I'm not that good at it.'

LOGIC

A girl said:
'I wrote myself a letter.'
So I said:
'What did it say?'
She said:
'I don't know.
I won't get it till tomorrow.'

A boy said:
'I'm really glad my mum called me Jack.'
I said:
'Why's that?'
He said:
'Because all the kids at school
call me that.'

PLAYING WITH WORDS

You can play with dice
You can play with cards
You can play with a ball
You can play with words
              words
              words
              words
              words
              words
              words
              banana
              words
              words
              words
              words
              words

FELT TIP

All over Naomi's bed
was felt tip
blobs
squiggles
shapes
and smudges.

Geraldine showed it to Laura.

That's naughty, Laura,
You mustn't do it.
You mustn't draw on Naomi's bed
do you hear me?
You
must
not
draw
on
Naomi's bed.

All right mummy,
Laura said,
I'll draw on my bed.

GEORGE

George said:
sometimes my dad doesn't shave
and his face is all prickly.

The new teacher said:
what does your mother say about that?

And George didn't say anything.

Clare said:
his mum don't live with his dad.

And the new teacher said:
Don't say don't
say doesn't.

And Clare said:
I live with my auntie.

CONVERSATION BETWEEN THREE CHILDREN

my mum and dad
scream at each other
sometimes
especially just before
mum throws a plate

my mum and dad
get sulky with each other
sometimes
especially just after
dad hasn't done the washing up

my mum and dad
don't scream at each other
don't get sulky with each other
don't live with each other

THE MICHAEL ROSEN RAP

You may think I'm happy, you may think I'm sad,
You may think I'm crazy, you may think I'm mad,
But hang on to your seats and listen right here
I'm gonna tell you something that'll burn your ear.

A hip. Hop. A hip hop hap.
I'm givin' you all the Michael Rosen rap.

I was born on the seventh of May
I remember very well that awful day
I was in my mother, curled up tight
Though I have to say, it was dark as night.
Nothing to do, didn't have to breathe,
I was so happy, didn't want to leave.

Suddenly, I hear some people give a shout:
One push, Mrs Rosen, and he'll be out.
I'm tellin' you all, that was a puzzle to me,
I shouted out, 'How do you know I'm a "he"?'
The doctor shouted, 'Good Lord, he can talk.'
I popped out my head, said, 'Now watch me walk.'
I juked and jived around that room,
Balam bam boola, balam de ditty boom.

A hip. Hop. A hip hop hap.
I'm givin' you all the Michael Rosen rap.

When I was one, I swam the English Channel,
When I was two, I ate a soapy flannel,
When I was three, I started getting thinner,
When I was four, I ate the dog's dinner,
When I was five, I was in a band playing drums,
When I was six, I ate a bag of rotten plums.
When I was seven, I robbed a bank with my sister,
When I was eight, I became Prime Minister,
When I was nine, I closed all the schools,
When I was ten, they made me King of the Fools.

So that's what I am, that's what I be
With an M, with an I, with a K, with an E.
That's what I am, that's what I be
Mr Mike, Mr Michael, Mr Rosen, Mr Me.
A hip. Hop. A hip hop hap.
I'm givin' you all the Michael Rosen rap.

NO ONE IN

Sometimes you come home
and there's no one in.
There are no lights on
no food ready
no telly
no one laughing
no jokes
just you
on your own.

That's when my brain
starts doing things:
you know,
murderers and mad dogs stuff.

I'll tell you what I do.
When I open the door
I shove it really hard and fast
and it bangs against the wall
really loud
so if he's hiding behind the door
he'll get it right on the nose.

I never have got him
I'll tell you what did happen though.
The door handle
made a great big hole in the wall.

TIDY YOUR ROOM

They say
Tidy your room –
But I'm trying to kill a fly on the wall
with a rolled-up comic.

They say
I'm asking you to tidy your room –
but I'm trying to kill the fly
by squashing it with a chunk of plasticene.

They say,
I am now TELLING you to tidy your room –
and I'm rolling up bits of plasticene.

For the last time – TIDY YOUR ROOM
but I'm making a line of the rolled-up bits of plasticene
along the edge of the chair.

They say,
Can you hear me?
I say, Yes.
I'm now flicking the bits of plasticene
at the fly on the wall.
They say,
What have we just asked you to do?
And I say,
I don't know.

PUZZLE I

She said I said he lied
but I said she said he lied
then you said she said I said he lied.

He said he didn't lie.

PUZZLE II

He was so tempted
he couldn't help himself
so he helped himself.

HEADACHE

It's a lump in your head
it's the blade of a knife
it's your veins bursting
it's your skull squeezing your brain
it's a headache.

THE GRINNERS BOOK OF RECORDS

The naughtiest girl in the world, Samantha Jones, was expelled from school for 92 years.

"DANGER KEEP CLEAR!"

"What's on television?"

"The aerial mate."

I THINK

I think
it's really bad news
they don't put paper
in our school loos.

If you need paper
you have to ask
right in front
of everyone in class.

You may think
I'm a bit of a fool
but that's why
I don't go to school.

TOMATO 1

Here's me
and my mum's just given me
a tomato.
And if there's one thing
I can't stand
it's
tomatoes.
You know that fleshy bit
the way it sticks to your teeth
and you know all those slimy little seeds,
the way they slide around your mouth,
ooh
I can't stand it.

Any way,
my mum says,
Eat it.
And I say,
Don't want to.
She says,
Eat it.
And I say,
I hate tomatoes, all slimy.
And she says,
Don't you talk like that
when I was a girl
I had to eat whatever my mum
put in front of me
do you think I could talk to my mother like that?
Do you know there are some people in the world
who'd give their right arm to have a tomato –
to have *half* a tomato –
because they haven't had anything to eat
for a whole week.
I'm telling you this,
if you don't eat your tomato
there'll be no afters
and I've made something Rather Nice,
I think you know what I mean . . .'

So here goes:
In goes a bit of tomato
Just like I thought.
First the fleshy bit.
It sticks.
Then the slimy bits
they slide about.
And when it all goes down my throat
it's
stick and slide
all the way down.
Oh no.
This is horrible.
So I start to
sulk.

I make my eyes go dim.
I push my lips out
to make myself look all rotten.
Don't you dare sulk, she says
I'm not having you sitting there
throwing one of your tantrums.
I don't have to put up with you behaving like this.
All I'm asking you to do
is eat one tomato.
It's taken months to grow.
It's full of goodness
and stop that stupid sulking, will you.

But I just sit there
in my great big sulk.

I never did eat that tomato.
Mind you,
I never got any afters either.

TOMATO 2: OR HOW I'VE LEARNT TO LOVE TOMATOES

When I get in
if there's one thing I love
it's a fat red tomato.
I love the feel of my tongue and lips
on the tight skin.
Then I make my teeth
cut into the flesh
so the juice jumps into my mouth
the coolness
and
the wetness.
So now I get some salt
and put a few grains on the flesh
so with my next bite
a tasty feel starts under my tongue.

So I get a piece of bread
and all the wheaty mealy stuff
mixes with all the juicy tomato stuff
and that's the way it goes down now
bread and tomato
tomato and bread
in a lovely
wet grainy savoury flavoury
round the mouth
fruity bready mush.

MY MUM'S MUM AND MY DAD'S DAD

My mum's mum and my dad's dad
met my mum's dad and my dad's mum
my mum's daughter and my dad's son
met my dad and met my mum.

How's your dad?
Not so bad.

All right mate?
Feeling great.

You OK?
Can't say.

Not ill again?
Can't complain.

How's your head?
Half dead.

QUIET PLEASE

No need to shout
no need to yell
no need to have a riot.
Shut your eyes
take a deep breath
ooh, you've gone all quiet!

TOE NAILS

More and more people in Britain today
are using
TOE-NAILS

Smart and smooth
they grow
on all five toes of each foot.

We spoke to Jack Davis of Hackney:
'Yes, I like toe-nails.
I've got ten of them.
Big ones for the big toes
and little ones for the little toes.
They're great.'

Be like Jack.
Be smart.
Grow toe-nails.

The Grinners Book of Records

The worlds most dangerous snail was called "King" Simon.

"I'm on Television."

TELLY

Put your thumb in the air
put your other finger out straight
take your other thumb
and put it on the end of your finger
and put your other finger
on the end of your thumb.

You've got a telly.

Put your ear on the telly

that programme's called
'What's this 'ere?'

Put your cheek on the telly

that programme's called
'Don't be cheeky.'

Put your nose on the telly

that programme's called
'The Nine o'clock Nose.'

USELESS INFORMATION

I read in a book that
Giraffes have no voices
The Red Sea is blue
Gorillas can't swim
Black treacle is brown
Elephants can't jump, and
Nothing rhymes with orange.

Does it?

MY MIND TOOK ME

My mind took me walking
walking down the street
took me to the lamp post
lamp post made of meat
took me to the gutter
gutter made of butter
took me to the trees
trees made of peas
hey you, Mind, I said
the pavement's sticky,
the pavement's tricky
it's made of toffee.

My mind took me walking
walking down the street
round my flats
my flats were a treat
with ice cream floors
and chocolate doors
I said, Hey Wow!
I'm hungry now.

So my mind took me walking
walking down my street
hot dog man gave me a hot dog to eat
that hot dog wasn't much good
hot dog sausage was a lump of wood.

So I took my mind walking
walking down the street
and I chucked my mind
in the dustbin.

EILEEN

my name is Eileen Ogle
and I run a dancing school
my name is Eileen Ogle
and my sister is a fool
my name is Eileen Ogle
I teach little girls to dance
my name is Eileen Ogle
and I'm living in a trance.

MY DAD CALLS ME

When I tell fibs
my dad calls me
Louis Lou Liar.

When I come in from playing
with my clothes a bit mucked up
he calls me
Dopey Dog Dirt.

When we were in this cafe
on holiday
and I laughed
and coughed orange juice all over the floor
my dad called me
Garry Gobhound.

When I watch telly
all Saturday morning
and I get a bit dozy
my dad calls me
Wally Tellybrains.

When my nose is a bit runny
and I can't find my hanky
my dad calls me
King of the Bogies.

I call him
Nag Bag.

I WENT

I went to a world
where blue dogs
licked my legs
and I lost my way
because my feet went invisible
but my nose turned gold
so I sold it for a million pounds
and with the money
I bought my ticket
back to tea-time
and it was
purple cheese on toast again.

FAST FOOD

A hamburger sat in a hamburger bar
waiting to be fried
'No one's going to put me,' it said,
'into anyone's inside.'

'Eating me is cruel;
eating me is murder.
You can't catch me
I'm The Speedy Hamburger.'

So up jumped the hamburger
and ran out of the bar.
'Hey come back here,' said Hamburger Cook,
'you won't get very far.'

But Hamburger rolled out of the door
and off down the street.
Who do you think was the first person
Hamburger happened to meet?

Lollipop Lady was walking home
with her lollipop in her hand.
'Get out of the way,' Hamburger yelled,
'I'm the fastest in the land.'

'Catch that hamburger!'
the cook yelled out.
So Lollipop Lady turned
and gave Hamburger a shout:

'Hey, little Hamburger,
you can't run away.'
But as Hamburger rushed past
he just had time to say:

'Eating me is cruel;
eating me is murder.
You can't catch me
I'm The Speedy Hamburger.'

Hamburger Cook and Lollipop Lady
ran off down the street.
And who do you think was the *next* person
Hamburger happened to meet?

Lemonade Boy with Lemonade bottles
was loading up the van
when Hamburger rushed past, shouting,
'I'm the fastest in the land.'

'Catch that hamburger,' said Hamburger Cook,
'it's trying to run away.'
'We're going to catch the little . . .'
Lollipop Lady began to say.

'I'll catch it,' said Lemonade Boy,
'I'm really fast.'
But just then he heard Hamburger shout
as it went hurtling past:

'Eating me is cruel;
eating me is murder.
You can't catch me
I'm The Speedy Hamburger.'

So Hamburger Cook and Lollipop Lady
followed by Lemonade Boy
ran off up the street
shouting, 'Hamburger Ahoy!'

And Hamburger rolled and Hamburger ran
and Hamburger couldn't be caught
and Hamburger rolled and Hamburger ran
right into an airport.

'Stop right there,' said Security Guard.
'Where do you think you're trying to go?'
'I'm just a little hamburger,' it said
'and I don't know where to go.'

For a moment it stood in front of the Guard
and then it darted past.
'You won't catch me,' it shouted
'you can't run very fast.'

'Eating me is cruel;
eating me is murder.
You can't catch me
I'm The Speedy Hamburger.'

Hamburger rolled through the terminal
and out on to the runway.
It ran up to a plane for Jamaica
that was waiting to get away.

The aeroplane took off
and flew into the air
and all the people heard something
as they were standing there:

'Eating me is cruel;
eating me is murder.
You can't catch me
I'm The Speedy Hamburger.'

MY MUM

My mum said to me and my brother:
'Don't crumble your bread or roll in the soup.'
I said:
'I don't want to roll in my soup.'

Then she said:
'Eat up, Michael.'
And my brother said:
'I don't want to eat up Michael.'

ZOO CAGE

let
me
out

WISE WORDS FROM DOCTOR SMARTYPANTS:

Many of you go to sleep, don't you?
That's what you do when you go to bed, isn't it?
Well, here's a little tip from me.
One that not many people know about.

When you get into bed
and you want to go to sleep . . .
SHUT YOUR EYES.

One little problem here:
when you wake up,
don't forget to . . .
OPEN YOUR EYES

Then you won't walk about all day
bumping into things.

Bye for now.

DR SMARTYPANTS

MORE WISE WORDS FROM DR SMARTYPANTS

The mouth
is the best place to put food and drink.
Don't try and put your food or drink
any higher than your mouth
or you'll find yourself
sticking your dinner in your eye.

And don't put it too low down
or you'll pour it all down your jumper.
So don't forget
Eat with your mouth.

Bye

THE SKYFOOGLE

There was a man
who turned up round our way once
put up a tent in the park, he did.
Put up notices all round the streets saying
that he was going to put on show
A TERRIFYING CREATURE!!!!!!
Called:
THE SKYFOOGLE!!!!!!!
No one had ever seen this thing before.
The show was on for
2 o'clock the next day.

Next day, we all turned up to see
THE FIERCEST ANIMAL IN THE WORLD!!!!!!!!!
The man took the money at the door
we all poured into the tent.
There was a kind of stage up one end
with a curtain in front of it.
We all sat down and waited.
The man went off behind the curtain.
Suddenly we all heard a terrible scream.
There was an awful yelling and crying,
there was the noise of chains rattling
and someone shouting.
Suddenly the man came running on to the stage
in front of the curtains.
All his clothes were torn,
there was blood on his face
and he screamed:
Quick, get out
get out
get out of here,
THE SKYFOOGLE HAS ESCAPED!!!!!!!

The Skyfoogle

We all got up
and ran out the door
and got away as fast as we could.

By the time we got ourselves together
the man had gone.
We never saw him again.
None of us ever saw our money again either . . . . . .
And none of us have ever seen THE SKYFOOGLE!!!!

SHRAM AND SHEDDLE

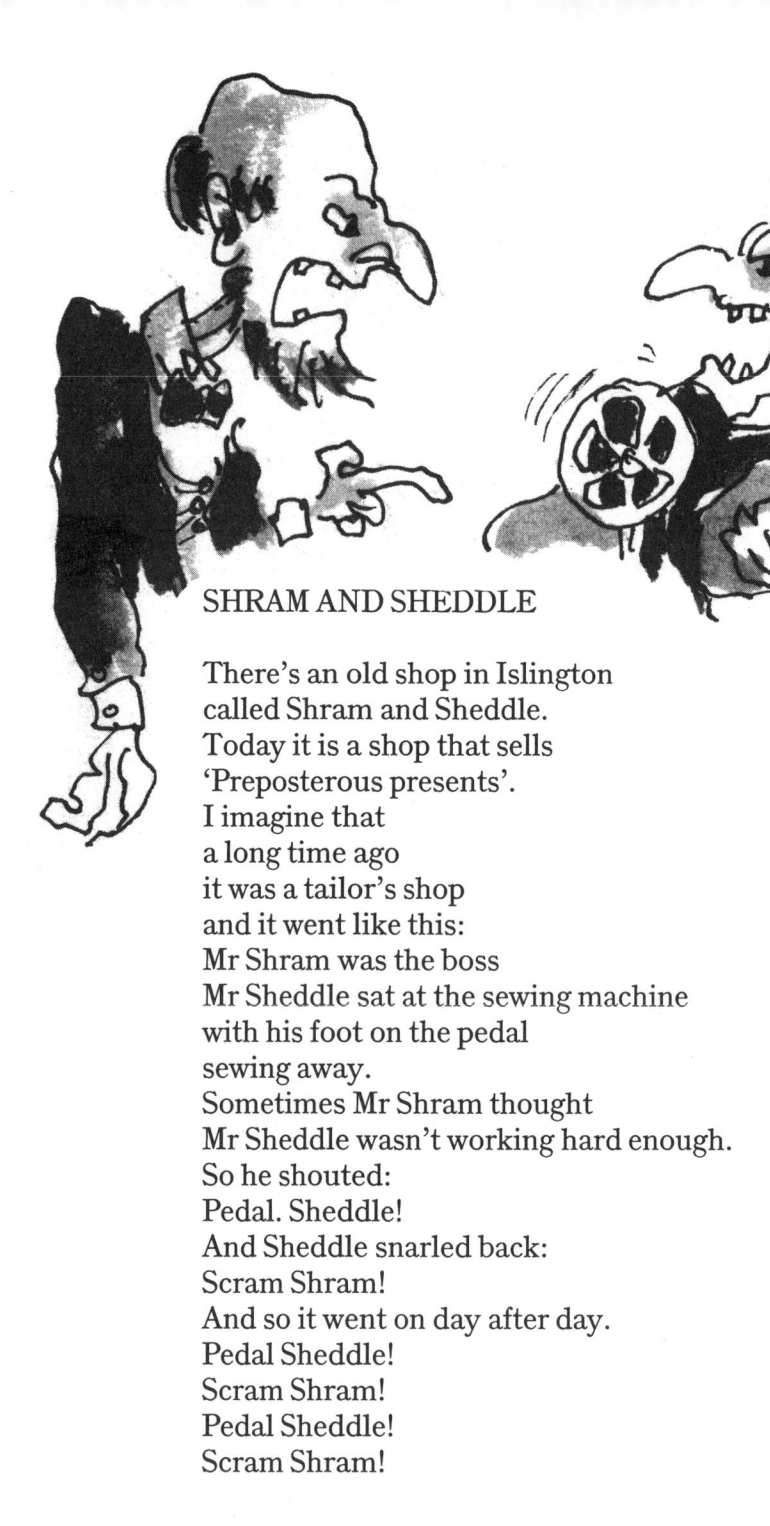

There's an old shop in Islington
called Shram and Sheddle.
Today it is a shop that sells
'Preposterous presents'.
I imagine that
a long time ago
it was a tailor's shop
and it went like this:
Mr Shram was the boss
Mr Sheddle sat at the sewing machine
with his foot on the pedal
sewing away.
Sometimes Mr Shram thought
Mr Sheddle wasn't working hard enough.
So he shouted:
Pedal. Sheddle!
And Sheddle snarled back:
Scram Shram!
And so it went on day after day.
Pedal Sheddle!
Scram Shram!
Pedal Sheddle!
Scram Shram!

GREAT MOMENTS IN HISTORY

1966, England wins world cup....

What we saw......

what the camera missed....

HARRYBO

Once my friend Harrybo
came to school crying.

We said:
What's the matter?
What's the matter?
And he said
his granddad had died.

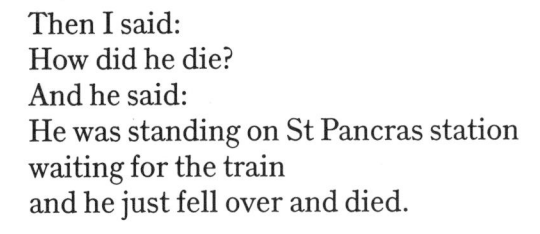

So we didn't know what to say.

Then I said:
How did he die?
And he said:
He was standing on St Pancras station
waiting for the train
and he just fell over and died.

Then he started crying again.

He was a nice man
Harrybo's grandad.
He had a shed with tins full of screws in it.

Mind you,
my gran was nice too
she gave me and my brother
a red shoe horn each.

Maybe Harrybo's grandad gave
Harrybo a red shoe horn.

Dave said:
My hamster died as well.
So everyone said:
Shhhh.
And Dave said:
I was only saying.
And I said:
My gran gave me a red shoe horn.

Rodge said:
I got a pair of trainers for Christmas.
And Harrybo said:
You can get ones without laces.
And we all said:
Yeah, that's right, Harrybo, you can.

Any other day,
we'd've said:
Of course you can, *we* know that, you fool.
But that day
we said:
Yeah, that's right, Harrybo, yeah, you can.

THE BUMP

I'm in the middle of a wrestle
with my brother
and I find my face
right up close to his ear
and then I see
THE BUMP.
THE BUMP is just next to his ear.
It's all shiny
and when you press it
it goes in like a push button
He says it doesn't hurt.
It just sits there.
THE BUMP.

Mum said that when he was born
it wasn't a bump
it was a shtickel.
I said, 'What's a shtickel?'
'Like a little stick,' she said,
'sticking out of the side of his head.'
She said they tied it up with a bit of cotton
and it died
until all that was left
was
THE BUMP.
The little shiny bump.

SPOTS IN MY EYES

I've got spots in my eyes.
Not spots *you* can see
they're on my side,
I see them when I'm looking at you.

To start with
I thought it was dirty windows,
then
I thought it was little flies in the air
but it isn't.
It's spots in my eye.

I'm trying to find out
where the spots are
in my eye.
If you see me staring at a white wall
trying to make one eye look at the other eye
that's what I'm doing
looking for the spots.
Actually I don't know what an eye is.
Maybe it's a plastic ball.
Or it's a kind of little round fish tank,
glass outside
water inside
and the spots are floating around
in the fish tank of my eye.

I wish I could get rid of them.
When people look up at the sky and say,
'Look at that – not a cloud in sight.'
I look up too
and there is all that blue sky
and there,
floating across all that blue
are
THE SPOTS.

MISTAKES

On my new super wizzo electric typewriter
there's a thing called
a correcting tape.
If you make a mistake,
what you do is
press this button that's got an 'X' on it
and the machine goes backwards
jumps up and peels the wrong letter
off the page.
It's great.

After a while
after you've made loads of mistakes
and you've used the correcting ribbon
a lot,
the ribbon runs out.
You have to take it off
and put a new one on.

I look at the old ribbon
and all the mistakes are stuck to it,
where the ribbon peeled them off the page.
It's like the ribbon has remembered
all my mistakes,
and you can sit and look at them,
all there in a long line
stuck to the ribbon.

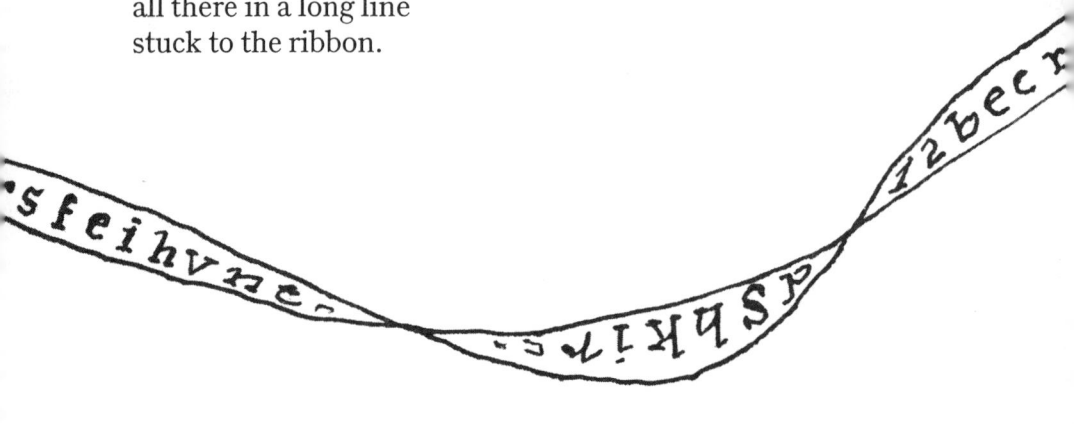

Hey,
what if you could have a correcting ribbon
for all the mistakes you ever made?
Like the time you called the teacher, 'Mummy'
and everyone laughed,
and the time you lied about sticking pins in the lipstick
and really awful things
like the time you screamed at your mum,
'I don't like you. No one likes you. Not even Dad.'

And all these mistakes
were on some correcting ribbon
and you could take it out of your drawer
and look at them.
I'd feel really terrible looking at all mine.

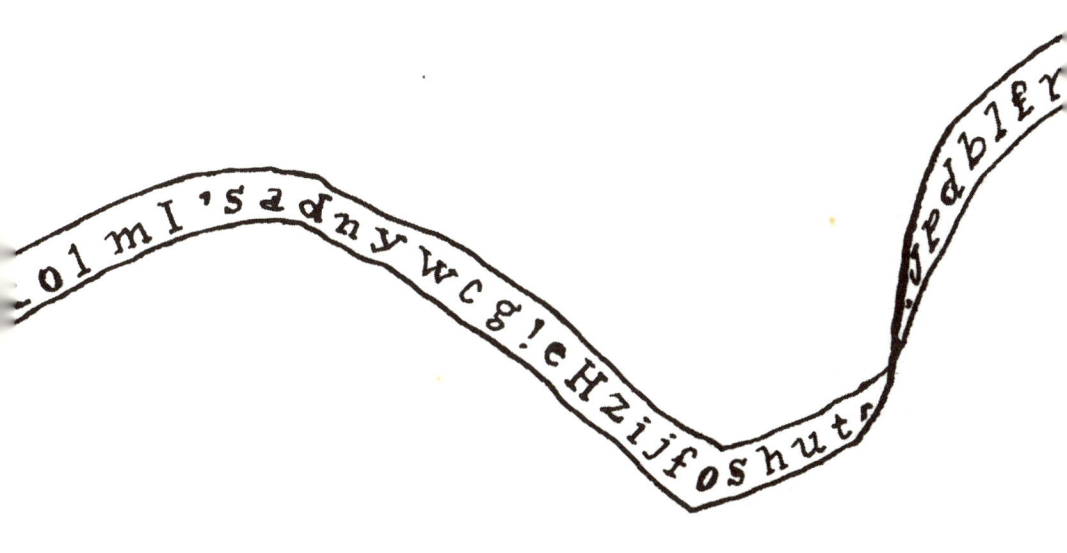

LAURA AND DOLLY

Laura who is two
was sitting on the stairs
playing with her doll.
Geraldine, her mum, was talking to Penny, the neighbour.
Suddenly they noticed a pool of something.
It was on the step –
just where Laura was sitting.
Perhaps Laura's doll was a bit wet from the bath,
Geraldine thought.
The pool got bigger and bigger.
It was coming from underneath Laura.
There was no question about it now.
It was wee.
Geraldine and Penny looked at Laura.
Laura looked at *them*
and said:
Dolly did it.